# Table of Contents

Drugged Driving Expert Panel Report:
A Consensus Protocol for Assessing the Potential of Drugs to Impair Driving

## Background

The recently published *2007 National Roadside Survey of Alcohol and Drug Use by Drivers: Drug Results* reported the drug prevalence (detected by oral fluid and blood samples) in 7,719 weekend drivers who served as participants in the survey (Lacey et al., 2009). The prevalence of drugs in drivers tested during the daytime was 11%.[1] Specifically, 5.8% tested positive for the category of illegal drugs, 4.8% for the medication category (i.e., prescription [Rx] and over-the-counter [OTC] medications), and 0.5% for the combined illegal and medication category. The nighttime survey results showed a prevalence of 14.4% for positive drug results. In this sample, 10.5% were positive for illegal drugs, 3% positive for the medication category, and 0.9% positive for the combined illegal and medication category. In addition, for those individuals who tested positive for illegal drugs (9.8%) the rate of those who also tested positive for alcohol was 28%. One of the major conclusions and recommendations of this study is that "further research is needed to determine the effect of drug prevalence on crash risk" (p.8).

In 2000, the National Transportation Safety Board (NTSB) recommended that the U. S. Department of Transportation (DOT) establish a list of approved medications and classes of medications that may be used safely when operating a vehicle (NTSB, 2000). The NTSB recommended that the DOT develop, "with assistance from experts on the effects of pharmacological agents on human performance and alertness, a list of approved medications." In its report, the NTSB stated that it had investigated over 100 accidents in all modes of passenger transportation that involved Rx or OTC medications whose effects could impair vehicle operators. The report states that most potentially impairing prescription or over-the-counter medications have significant cognitive effects. The NTSB expressed concern that vehicle operators using such medications might not always be in a position to accurately judge the extent and effect of such impairment: "a vehicle operator whose judgment is adversely affected by a medication may decide, inappropriately, that he or she is not impaired." The NTSB found that there was "relatively little regulatory guidance available from the DOT, its modal administrations, the FDA, or other regulatory agencies for vehicle operators with regard to use of over-the-counter and prescription medications."

In the years following these NTSB recommendations, a number of drug lists have been developed by DOT. In 2004, the National Highway Traffic Safety Administration (NHTSA) released a report (Couper & Logan, 2004) titled, *Drugs and Human Performance Fact Sheets*. This was the report of a panel of international experts, reviewing developments over the preceding 10 years in identifying the specific effects of illicit and prescription drugs on driving. The fact sheets represent the "current scientific knowledge in the area of drugs and human performance for the 16 drugs selected for examination" (Couper & Logan, 2004, p.1). Although the fact sheets are uniform in organization, the studies determining the impact on driving, listed under the headings, "Performance Effects" and "Effects on Driving," are not uniform, but reflect

---

[1] The daytime data collection was comprised of oral fluid samples; nighttime data collection involved both oral and blood samples.

a myriad of study methodologies. A similar effort is the National Institute on Drug Abuse (NIDA, 2007) chart listing called *Commonly Abused Drugs*. Shinar (2005) described NIDA's efforts as "laudable attempts to synthesize the results of very many and methodologically different studies into a few paragraphs that are simple to understand" (p. 55). Unfortunately, this necessitates some generalizations that are often not very accurate, and often describe the effects of different drug categories in the same or similar terms, making them indistinguishable from each other." Similar efforts in the European Union (Maes, Charlier, Grenez, & Verstraete, 1999) generated lists of "Drugs and medicines that are suspected to have a detrimental impact on road user performance." These too were based on compilation of existing epidemiological, laboratory-based, and over-the-road driving studies. In 2003, NHTSA published a review of the *State of Knowledge of Drug-Impaired Driving* (Jones, Shinar, & Walsh, 2003) covering literature published since 1980. The report indicates areas for which the authors could find no experimental research (e.g., hallucinogens and inhalants), drugs for which there is a high potential for significant impairment of driving following acute administration (e.g., narcotics, long-acting benzodiazepines at therapeutic doses, short-acting benzodiazepines at high doses, barbiturates, first-generation antihistamines, and tricyclic antidepressants), and drug classes with "relatively low potential for significant impairment after acute usage" (e.g., CNS stimulants, and second-generation $H_1$ antihistamines). The report states that "very few studies have examined the chronic and sub-chronic use of the above classes of drugs, and most of those that have suggest little effect on driving and driving-related performance."

**The Drugged Driving Expert Panel**
In November 2008 and again in March 2009, an expert panel was convened by NHTSA with the goal of determining whether a list could be developed, indicating which medications or classes of medications may pose a hazard to driving. There was particular interest in having the panel develop a list of "safe" medications that do not impair driving. The value of the list would be to better inform patients and physicians regarding the likely effects of a drug on driving. This information could lead to better-informed prescribing practices and to more rational selection of medications by patients.

The panel was composed of an international group of behavioral scientists, epidemiologists, pharmacologists, toxicologists, and traffic safety professionals to provide a broad-based perspective on the issue. Discussions included Rx medications as well as OTC medications and illicit drugs. Although illicit drugs are best known for their impairing effects, Rx and OTC medications are also known to be capable of producing impairment and many are frequently encountered in impaired-driver populations.

There was agreement among the panel that a limited number of drugs generally pose a low risk to driving when taken according to approved prescribing information and when used with appropriate medical oversight. However, the panel also recognized that even among drugs generally considered safe for driving, adverse reactions may occur, and interactions may occur between these medications and other drugs or alcohol that could impair driving performance. The panel was of the opinion that some specific drugs and drug classes are clearly impairing, including sedatives, hypnotics, sedating antihistamines, narcotic analgesics, hallucinogens, antipsychotics, and muscle relaxants, even at therapeutic or sub-therapeutic doses. However, for many drug classes, the question of impairment falls in a grey area, either because the potential adverse effects are highly dose-dependent or because there is much heterogeneity within the class. For some of the impairing drugs in this group, it is likely that drug tolerance alone determines the extent of impairment. Examples of drugs that fall in this category include many selective serotonin reuptake inhibitor (SSRI) antidepressants, anticonvulsants, and antihypertensives.

The panel agreed that one of the barriers to categorizing drugs with respect to driving impairment risk is the *lack of a common, standardized protocol for assessing the impairing potential of drugs.* For most drugs, behavioral effects have not been studied systematically. For those drugs that have been studied, the evaluation of driving impairment risk is incomplete as a result of the inconsistency of testing methodologies employed and the use of research protocols that failed to address critical issues of dose, time since dosing, interaction between drug and condition being treated, and chronicity of use. Furthermore, the use of non-standardized testing methods has hindered comparison across studies.

The panel recognized the need for a structured, standardized protocol for assessing the driving-impairment risk of drugs. This approach would lead to better classification of drugs in terms of driving-impairment risk and would potentially be useful in providing more meaningful precautions for users and prescribers regarding the impacts of drugs on driving.

There was agreement among the panel that effective assessment methodologies currently are available that could be incorporated into a standardized protocol for assessing the driving impairment risk of drugs. The panel reviewed existing protocols including the recent guidelines proposed by International Council on Alcohol, Drugs, & Traffic Safety (Walsh, Verstraete, Heustis, & Mørland, 2008). This group similarly recognized that standardization of methodologies would allow for inter-study comparison and more uniform means of reporting effects. The panel's conclusion is that the optimum model for selecting and evaluating candidate drugs for comprehensive assessment would result from a tiered, parallel process involving pharmacological, toxicological, epidemiological reviews and a standardized behavioral assessment (based on the Essential Driving Ability Domains [EDAD] model).

## Tiered Assessment Protocol

The approach proposed by the panel, a tiered, parallel process, consisting of pharmacological/toxicological, and epidemiological reviews, and a standardized behavioral assessment is shown in Figure 1. The components of the protocol and their interrelations, and the proposed procedure for validating the protocol are detailed in the following sections.

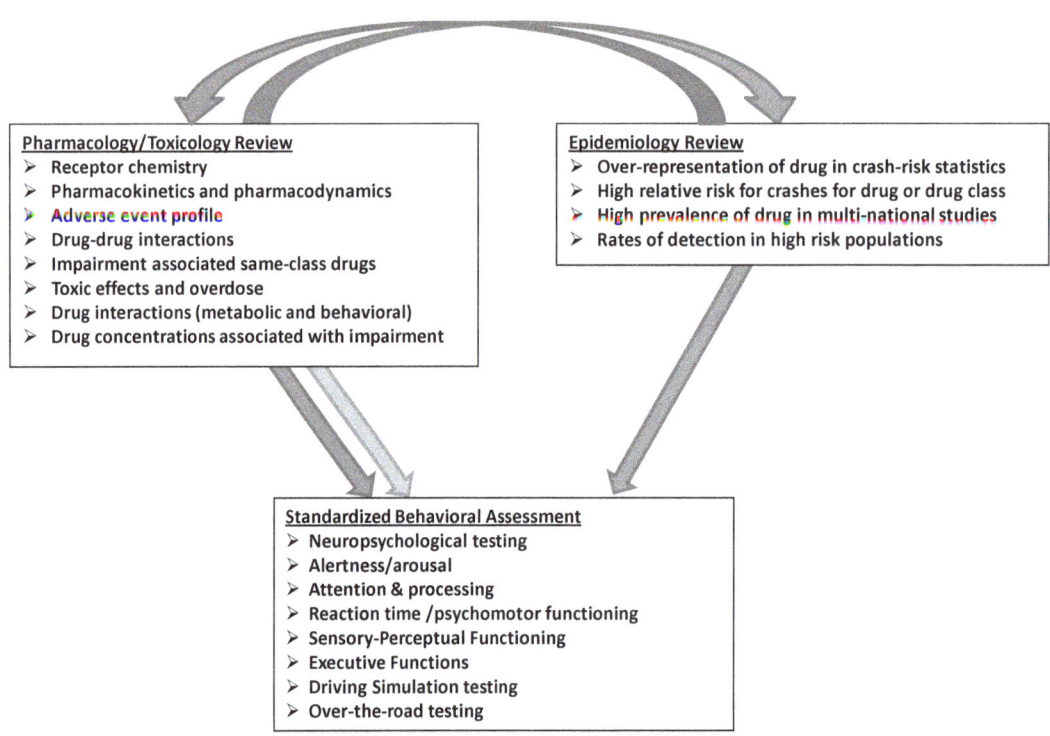

*Figure 1.* Interrelation of the pharmacological/toxicological, epidemiological and behavioral assessments proposed by the panel.

## Pharmacological and Toxicological Review

A drug can be flagged as being of concern, either through an empirical consideration of the *pharmacology* or the *toxicology* of the drug. The **pharmacological** review considers such factors as receptor chemistry, pharmacokinetics, pharmacodynamics, main effects (i.e., the drug's indications), and adverse event profiles. A drug can be compared on these parameters to other drugs within the same drug class. It can also be compared to other drug classes with similar characteristic side-effects. Based on the drug's physical chemistry and receptor chemistry, information a determination can be made as to the likelihood that the drug will cross the blood-brain barrier and occupy key receptors critical to the cognitive and/or psychomotor functions critical to driving. The pharmacological information can also be used to predict time to peak effect, duration of impairment, and the impact of drug-drug interactions. Pharmacological information will also provide information about subgroups in the population that might be at higher risk for drug impairment due to "deviating" pharmacokinetics such as often observed in the elderly or in those who are poor metabolizers.

Review of the **toxicology** literature can yield data on adverse events, abuse, overdoses, and drug interactions. Case reports can identify circumstances of drug use that have resulted in impaired driving, crashes, or arrests, sometimes including associated quantitative toxicological measurements in blood or oral fluid. Current toxicological literature contains case reports of specific sets of circumstances that can result in impairment, most notably specific drug concentrations, adverse reactions, and drug interactions that have been associated with impairment.

If the pharmacology and toxicology review indicates a risk for effects on driving, the epidemiological literature and databases would be searched for evidence of prevalence and magnitude that might assist in prioritizing drugs for the standardized behavioral assessment (blue arrows). Clearly, if a drug is in development or clinical trials and has not been prescribed, a drug candidate can be recommended for behavioral assessment without epidemiological evidence (green arrow).

**Epidemiological Review**
Following pharmacological and toxicological assessment, **epidemiological** literature would be reviewed to identify medical conditions associated with certain types of drug use, over-representation of certain drugs in crash-risk statistics, and, where possible, relative risk of impairment for drugs or drug classes, based either on comparison to control populations or by means of culpability assessment. Unfortunately, there are major gaps in the epidemiological literature. In a recently published report, Orriols and colleagues (2009) reviewed electronic databases between 1979 and 2008 for relevant epidemiological studies. Eligible studies had to evaluate the causal relationship between the use of medicinal drugs and the risk of traffic crashes. Twenty-two studies designed with different degrees of methodological rigor were included. According to the authors, "The risk of motor-vehicle crashes related to benzodiazepines has been amply studied and demonstrated. Results from other medicinal drugs remain controversial" (Abstract Results section, para. 3) Epidemiological evaluation will usually follow from toxicological and pharmacological concerns; however, it may serve as a unique indicator of concern, for unexpected side effects not predicted from the drugs main pharmacological profile. For example, a drug that might cause hypotension, but would not necessarily trigger a review based on toxicology/pharmacology, might show up in epidemiological data as a problem in older drivers. This would trigger a pharmacological/toxicological review (red arrows), leading to behavioral assessment.

**Standardized Behavioral Assessment**
Those drugs identified by the pharmacological/toxicology and epidemiological assessments as being likely to impair driving would be prioritized for evaluation by a **Standardized Behavioral Assessment**. The behavioral assessment protocol would incorporate sophisticated laboratory methods for assessing the cognitive, perceptual, and psychomotor effects of drugs. In addition, the behavioral assessment protocol would employ driving simulators and over-the-road driving tests in the assessment of crash risk. The behavioral assessment would be conducted at relevant doses and at various times post-dose to establish the time-course of impairment. The objective

of the behavioral assessment protocol would be to evaluate drugs with respect to their likelihood of impairing driving-related skills. The driving-related skills to be evaluated are those cognitive, perceptual, and psychomotor abilities known to be critical to the task of driving. These are described in the Essential Driving ability Domains Model

**The Essential Driving Ability Domains (EDAD) Model.** Driving is recognized to be a highly complex activity involving a wide range of cognitive, perceptual, and motor activities that take place in a complex, dynamic environment. Direct assessment of "driving" may be an aspirational goal, but for purposes of the present objective it is considered beyond current assessment technology. An alternative to the direct assessment of "driving" as a holistic, integrated behavior-in-context is the "part-task" assessment of driving-related abilities (or skills). This involves assessment of those abilities that are essential to the task of driving in a controlled (laboratory) setting. Though it is desirable, it is not always possible to include attributes during performance measurement that increase contextual (ecological) validity for driving. Decades of research on driving has identified various tasks involved in the performance of this activity; the most critical tasks (and the abilities that underlie them) are determined empirically through crash data analyses, where available, or through experimental studies in naturalistic, closed-course, or high-fidelity simulator settings. Performance of each of these driving tasks is dependent upon certain cognitive, perceptual, and motor abilities. Knowing the specific abilities required to perform a given task, as well as the level of that ability required to perform the task, allows for development of a test battery that is predictive of complex human performance (Fleishman, Quaintance, & Broedling, 1984) under defined conditions.

Driving-related skills and required abilities are typically described using constructs taken from various fields in psychology (e.g., cognitive psychology and neuropsychology) and human factors engineering. There are often multiple terms used to describe these ability categories depending upon the discipline providing the description. In some areas there are overlapping terms, while in others the same term may be used to describe an entirely different construct. The goal of the panel was to use the most widely accepted terminology and to carefully define terms. The terms used by the panel are consistent with those used in the fields of psychology, pharmacology, and medicine and therefore are considered appropriate for evaluating drug effects and communicating those results beyond transportation researchers.

The panel identified five behavioral domains relevant to driving: (1) alertness/arousal; (2) attention and processing speed; (3) reaction time/psychomotor functions; (4) sensory-perceptual functions; and (5) executive functions. The behavioral assessment protocol was designed to evaluate all five of these domains. A drug that impairs performance in any of these domains *at a magnitude known to be associated with increased crash risk* is presumed to have a negative impact on driving safety. Each of the five domains is described in the following sections. The measures, that were suggested by the panel to assess the characteristics of the respective domains, are listed as well.

*Essential driving ability domains.*
a) *Alertness/Arousal.* This refers to the individual's level of consciousness that can range from full alertness, to drowsiness, somnolence, stupor, and coma. According to Lezak (2004) the

slightest changes to the level of arousal may lessen one's "mental efficiency" which plays a factor in the development of inattention and fatigue.

Drowsiness is known to lead to impaired vigilance, increased weaving, poorer speed control, and, as a result, impaired driving performance. Driver drowsiness can lead to falling asleep while driving. Inadequate sleep and use of sedating drugs is a major cause of drowsiness related crashes.

*Measures:* Self-report (e.g., visual analog scales and sleepiness scales); laboratory performance measures (e.g., psychomotor vigilance testing); and sleep laboratory measures of daytime wakefulness (e.g., multiple sleep latency test, maintenance of wakefulness test). Due to the frequent lack of correspondence between self-report and other measures, these measures should only be used as an extension of objective, laboratory measures.

b) ***Attention and Processing Speed.*** There are a myriad of definitions of attention that share in common the idea that attention refers to the capacities or processes involved in becoming receptive to internal or external stimuli. There are a number of facets of attention recognized in the fields of neuropsychology and cognitive psychology, including; (1) focused or selective attention (which is commonly referred to as concentration); (2) sustained attention or vigilance (which refers to the ability to maintain attention over time); (3) divided attention (which refers to the ability to respond to more than one task at a time); (4) shifting or alternating attention (which refers to the ability to shift or modify the focus of attention), and (5) working memory (which refers to attentional capacity in terms of the amount of information that can be held in temporary storage when concentrating and which is susceptible to loss with time and/or distraction). Each of these five facets of attention appears to play an essential role in one or more driving tasks.

Information processing speed may affect the performance of all tasks beyond the sensory level. Processing speed changes occur with normal aging and may compound the effects of drugs.

*Measures*: Self-report (e.g., self-reported difficulty with concentration); laboratory testing of the specific facets of attention (e.g., tests of working memory, vigilance, focused attention, shifting attention, and divided attention); instrumented vehicle and driving simulator measures (including measures designed to assess eye movements and gaze). Self-report measures are not relied upon, but are used to assess subject awareness of changes in functioning.

c) ***Reaction Time/Psychomotor Functions.*** This construct refers to the speed of response as well as the coordination of skilled movement. Motoric response speed is a function of perceptual speed and response selection, plus the speed and coordination of the motor response. Perceptual speed may be diminished by peripheral or central sensory deficits. Similarly, psychomotor functions are controlled by central and peripheral factors that underlie neuromuscular function.

Although simple reaction time is not particularly predictive of driving performance, complex reaction time, which involves both response selection and perceptual sensitivity, is related to driving performance.

Vehicle control is dependent upon motor coordination and visual-motor abilities. The ability to appropriately apply the brakes of a vehicle is dependent upon psychomotor functions and perceptual speed. Similarly, the individual's ability to avoid a collision is dependent upon the speed with which they can begin implementing the appropriate action. While reaction time and psychomotor functions are essential, a much greater part of the variance in total response time for vehicle control actions is typically accounted for by the "choice" components (perceptual speed, response selection) than by the "simple" component (motor response speed).

*Measures:* Simple and complex reaction time tests, and driving simulator or over-the-road driving tasks (e.g., brake reaction time). Performance on psychomotor tasks (e.g., tests of upper motor speed and coordination) are also predictive of driving control.

d) ***Sensory-Perceptual Functioning.*** This term refers to the specific visual, auditory, proprioceptive, and sensorimotor abilities that enable the critical driving tasks. Sensory abilities need to be sufficient to perceive vehicle and roadway conditions, and to provide appropriate feedback to the operator about the consequences of vehicle control movements.

*Measures:* Examples include visual fields and perimetry testing, and contrast sensitivity.

e) ***Executive Functions.*** This term refers to those capacities that are involved in planning, approaching, organizing, monitoring, prioritizing and carrying out various cognitive activities. They relate to the individual's ability to control his/her behavior, to show control over impulses and to use "good judgment." Executive functions are considered to play a key role in driving as they impact upon the driver's planning, ability to avoid crashes, and assess risk.

*Measures:* The tests used to assess executive functions mostly originated from cognitive psychology and neuropsychology. They typically involve measures of mental flexibility, adaptive problem solving, abstract reasoning, impulse control, risk taking, organizational ability (including visuospatial organization), and planning. Instrumented vehicle measures of navigational performance may provide another indication of executive function.

From the EDAD model, the panel derived a comprehensive behavioral assessment test battery, to estimate the effects of drugs on driving.

**The Behavioral Assessment Test Battery**. Behavioral assessment of the effects of drugs on driving requires the use of a comprehensive test battery that evaluates the *Essential Driving Abilities Domains*. The panel agreed upon criteria for the inclusion of tests in the behavioral assessment test battery. The panel specified that the measures proposed for this protocol need to be standardized (e.g., having uniform procedures for administering and scoring the test and suitable, representative norms), have established reliability (e.g., consistent scoring across examiners and consistent results obtained upon re-administration), and documented validity (e.g., sensitivity, specificity, and demonstration that the test measures what it purports to measure). Useful guidelines for testing can be found in the Standards for Educational and Psychological Testing (American Psychological Association, & National Council on Measurement in Education, 1999). In addition to these criteria, the panel specified the following requirements for tests to be included in the battery:

- **They should be predictive of driving performance.** Tests of driving-related abilities that have been found to be predictive of driving performance (simulated or over-the-road driving) were considered to be optimal for inclusion in the test battery. The panel decided that unless there was at least some compelling association to driving safety outcomes a measure would not be included in the test battery.

- **They should demonstrate sensitivity to drug effects.** Selection among alternative tests found to be predictive of driving performance should be guided by the extent to which the published literature indicates the sensitivity of the candidate tests to either drugs of abuse or to pharmaceuticals. Preferably the test has been able to demonstrate sensitivity to more than one class of drugs known to impair driving. The sensitivity of the test to detecting drug effects would preferably be expressed in terms of the power of the test to detect a specified level of change in performance. Information on the power of the test is critical for study design (e.g., determining number of subjects needed for the study). Tests also need to be specific (i.e., have a low rate of false positive errors). The sensitivity and specificity of tests should be expressed in terms of positive predictive value (i.e., likelihood of impairment associated with a positive result).

- **They should include measures of sustained attention of sufficient duration to detect lapses of attention with operational significance for safe driving.** One of the major limitations frequently seen in published drug studies is the use of "sustained" attention tests that are too short in duration to demonstrate the effects of fatigue and monotony on drugged driving. Deficiencies in vigilance that impact driving performance may not be detected with task durations less than 20 minutes.

- **They should be suitable for inclusion in a comprehensive test battery.** Individual tests are administered as part of a comprehensive battery to fully characterize the behaviors (or abilities) that are impaired and/or not impaired by a particular drug. All of the identified domains should be tested, including each of the facets of attention plus processing speed (described on page 7). It is recognized that tests generally measure more than a single behavioral domain.

The test battery proposed by the panel is referred to as the *Consensus Test Battery for Assessing Impaired Driving Abilities* (see Appendix A). Similar test batteries have been constructed by neuropsychologists working with a number of neurological conditions including multiple sclerosis (Bever, Jr., Grattan, Panitch, & Johnson, 1995), schizophrenia (Nuechterlein et al, 2008), and for various dementias. Such test batteries represent a core that represent the minimum required tests to be administered in clinical trials. There are numerous advantages of having a standardized test battery. However, the panel wanted to make it clear that the test battery is not intended to be monolithic or to exclude the development of superior tools as they become available. In the future, final selection of instruments to be included in the test battery will be determined by another multidisciplinary panel of experts (e.g., in psychometrics, cognitive psychology, neuropsychology, statistics, and driving assessment). The specific list of generic and commercially available tests selected by this panel will be determined in the future. The specification of a limited number of tests within each of the specified domains will provide a far more standardized approach to evaluating impairment than has been used in the past.

**Driving Tests.** After identifying the essential driving ability domains and the requirements for the test battery, the next level of evaluation in this tiered approach to assessment of the effects of drugs on driving is the application of various driving tasks, including driving simulators, closed course driving studies, over-the-road driving studies, and the recent use of instrumented vehicles. The panel recommends these behavioral tests separately from the other behavioral test methods due to their added content (and face) validity in studying drug-related driving impairment.

All these methods have specific advantages and disadvantages for testing drug-related impairment of driving. For example, driving simulators can safely present relevant driving scenarios in a standardized and relatively low-cost manner. Driving simulators have been proven to be sensitive to stimulant and depressant central nervous system (CNS) drug effects in normal individuals and in patients. On the other hand, simulated driving does not present the same sensorimotor cues that exist in "real driving" and crashes obviously do not have the same consequences. Closed-course driving has been shown to be sensitive to various drug effects, but is lacking in realism, and has been found to be suitable for only a limited number of driving-related tasks (Jones, et.al. 2003). Over-the-road driving tasks (e.g., Verster et al., 2002), as exemplified by the Netherlands' CBR Driving Test which is conducted on a 100-kilometer stretch of highway, have been used to study weaving (standard deviation of lateral position), and vehicle following. These driving tasks have been shown to be sensitive to a wide range of drugs. However, as with closed-course driving studies there are a limited range of driving tasks that can be safely accomplished, and the driver's performance may be influenced by the presence of a driving instructor.

The panel recognized that for driving simulators, closed-course driving tests, and for over-the-road driving tests, there are measures that are known to be sensitive to drug effects and that are indicative of driving impairment. However, except for the CBR Driving Test, as conducted by laboratories in the Netherlands, there is very little standardization of these other driving tests. As a result, the current role for these other methods in the tiered protocol developed by the panel is limited. Nonetheless, PC-based driving simulators have proven sensitive to alcohol (Verster, et al., 2009), CNS depressants (Staner, et al., 2005), sleep deprivation (Gurtman, Broadbear, & Redman, 2008), and stimulants (Kay, Michaels, & Pakull, 2009). Recent studies conducted with the National Advanced Driving Simulator (Brown, Dow, Marshall, & Allen, 2007; Salaani, Heydinger, & Grygier, 2006; Senserrick, Brown, Quistberg, Marshall, & Winston, 2007) have shown comparable results for simulated driving and over-the-road driving.

Instrumented vehicles are anticipated to provide a naturalistic approach to studying driver behavior under everyday operating conditions and must also be considered. This may include prospective monitoring of populations following prescription of certain classes of drugs, or placing instrumentation including performance monitoring devices in vehicles to observe driving patterns over time. These approaches avoid some of the observation effect encountered in the laboratory model, and remove specific dosing controls, allowing assessment of individual subject practices of drug administration (missed doses, double doses, changes in dose, etc.) not possible in a laboratory environment.

The outcomes of interest include crashes (both injurious and noninjurious) and explicit observable errors in performance recognized as a factor in crash causation through a consensus of those knowledgeable in the field. Such errors include encroachment into an opposite-direction-of-travel lane; disregard of a traffic control device controlling vehicle movements at an intersection; collisions with roadway geometric features (curbs, medians); driving at a speed that is inappropriate for conditions or that deviates significantly from that of other traffic; driving in a manner that requires overt evasive actions on the part of other motorists or pedestrians to avert a collision; and loss of consciousness while driving.

Naturalistic driving studies using instrumented vehicles do not provide experimental control, but do provide the most naturalistic observation of drivers under "real-world" driving conditions. In a recent NHTSA report, Staplin, Lococo, Gish, and Martel (2008) employed instrumented vehicles in a small sub-sample of the subjects (n=5). Differences were seen between drives completed when the driver was alone or when accompanied by an occupational therapist. To date, there are no known controlled studies using instrumented vehicles to assess drug effects during naturalistic driving. However, the use of unobtrusive, affordable, miniature, in-car instrumentation packages suggests that this type of research is becoming feasible.

**Study Design Methodology.** The panel addressed the specifics of the drug testing protocol. Assessment of driving impairment risk requires testing at relevant doses with assessment of initial dose effects as well as steady-state dosing effects. It is considered important to test drugs at their peak CNS level (which does not always correspond to the time to maximum drug plasma concentration concentration, referred to as TMAX) and to also assess potential withdrawal effects. The study design should generally include comparator drugs (e.g., placebos and known non-impairing drug from the same drug class) as well as a positive control to demonstrate the sensitivity of the testing methodology. Studies can be conducted with healthy, young subjects to provide information about the effects of a drug independent of the effects of the disease or symptoms for which the drug is taken. However, use of these subjects may lead to an under-estimation or overestimation of drug effects, and may fail to differentiate the impact of the underlying disease condition (or relief of symptoms) from the effect of the drug. Therefore, the panel recognizes that studies need to be conducted with both relevant patient groups and with normal healthy control subjects. In all cases the characteristics of the study subjects should be described in detail. The panel provided guidelines on the training of subjects to perform the test battery. Of particular concern is the need for obtaining a stable baseline performance level and the need to minimize practice effects that can obscure drug effects. The panel also recognizes that overly frequent administration of a test can result in the test becoming "over-practiced" and failing to assess the intended construct.

The protocol stresses the need for an *a priori* statistical analysis plan. Endpoints need to be defined prior to any data analysis. Studies need to be adequately powered to detect a meaningful change in the endpoint. The panel encouraged calibration of test results relative to alcohol. There is a wealth of literature demonstrating dose-related effects of alcohol on driving and on crash risk. Particularly for CNS depressants it may be useful to present findings *relative to specific blood alcohol levels.* For other drug categories such as stimulants, alcohol may be a less appropriate comparator.

## Validation of the Tiered Assessment Protocol

The panel recommended a process for validating the tiered protocol. The first step is application of the pharmacological/epidemiological/toxicological process to identify a small number of candidate drugs known to impair driving. These drugs would then be subjected to the behavioral assessment protocol.

Initial validation of the consensus test battery could be accomplished by testing one or two prototype drugs from among the classes of drugs known to impair driving (opiates, cannabinoids, benzodiazepines, cocaine, amphetamines, and barbiturates). The selected drugs should be tested alone and in combination with alcohol. Medications should be tested at doses representing the full therapeutic range of dosing. Testing should be conducted to assess both acute and steady-state dosing effects, and at relevant time intervals post-dosing (to establish the time course of impairment as well as the effects of withdrawal). Drugs should be tested at peak serum level ($T_{max}$) as well as at times known or suspected to be associated with maximum impairment. The validation studies should include a representative sample of individuals of the target population. Although the individual tests that comprise the consensus test battery, by definition are all validated instruments, it will be necessary to empirically validate the test battery as a whole. This process involves careful examination of the intercorrelations between the tests and specifically a determination of the convergent and discriminant validity of the measures.

The panel provided specific guidelines for conducting the validation process:
*(1) A qualified institutional review board should review all studies.* All research with the proposed battery should follow applicable legal and ethical guidelines.
*(2) Drug studies should include a collection of blood samples*. This will allow the study to assess behavioral effects relative to drug concentrations. Sufficient time-separated blood samples should be collected to establish the pharmacokinetic profile as well as the behavioral profile of impairment associated with the administered drug. Blood analysis should be performed according to procedures with uniform performance characteristics of precision, accuracy, sensitivity and scope and should include measurement of active metabolites.
*(3) Performance should be assessed relative to the subject's baseline.* Prior to obtaining a baseline level of performance (pre-dosing) subjects should receive adequate training on the test battery to achieve a stable, repeatable level of performance.
*(4) Treatment and/or order of treatment should be randomized.* Regardless of whether the study design involves parallel groups or a cross-over design, subjects and treatment orders need to be randomized with respect to treatment.
*(5) Data management practices should be consistent with those employed in pharmaceutical research.* Data collection and monitoring practices should be conducted in accordance with practices employed in current pharmaceutical research (International Conference on Harmonisation, 2005).

The results of the validation process should lead to a report on the observed statistical power of each of the tests and of the full test battery to detect a specified level of change in performance, with anticipated consequences for vehicle control and safety. Statistically significant changes in performance may or may not be associated with operationally significant changes in safety. These findings would be valuable for the design of subsequent studies.

## Application of the Tiered Assessment Protocol: Examples

### Cannabis

If the protocol was to be applied to the study of *cannabis*, the process would begin with an assessment of the pharmacology and toxicology of *cannabis*.

**Tier I: Pharmacological and toxicological review.** The active component of marijuana/*cannabis* is delta-9-tetrahydrocannabinol (THC). THC interacts with CB1 receptors in the brain, causing a variety of effects on organ systems and is believed to be related to the drugs ability to cause hallucinations and changes in sensory perception. Other adverse effects associated with THC use include paranoia, panic, and orthostatic hypotension, all of which may affect psychomotor performance and cognitive skills. The drug is known to cross the blood brain barrier and has been confirmed by PET scans to affect brain areas critical for motor control and visual processing (Bossong et al., 2009).

**Tier II: Epidemiological review.** THC is commonly detected in drivers and is frequently the most common drug after alcohol found in the blood of at risk driving populations (drivers arrested for impaired driving, and fatally injured drivers; Jones et al., 2003; Drummer et al., 2004). Some studies suggest that relative risk ratios are not significantly elevated, however methodologically many of these suffer by not taking into account the time of driving relative to the time of sample collection, and the rapid redistribution kinetics of THC. The toxicology literature would show that this is one of the more common drugs found in fatal crashes (Drummer et al., 2004).

**Tier III: Standardized behavioral assessment.** Based on the pharmacological/toxicological and epidemiological review, THC would be a priority candidate for behavioral assessment and would progress to the behavioral testing phase of the protocol. Prior research has identified doses of *cannabis* expected to produce changes in attention, motor skills and executive functions. Based on the epidemiological and toxicological reviews, evaluation of cannabis effects could proceed at drug concentrations commonly seen in drivers or could be conducted at levels above and below the level currently considered to be a threshold for impairment. The testing would be conducted in a well-defined population of drug users using an IRB approved protocol and conducted in a facility experienced in conducting research with illicit drugs. Subjects would be trained on the consensus test battery and once having established a baseline would be administered *cannabis* at the specified doses. Testing would be conducted at specified times post-dosing and blood samples would be taken to evaluate the relationship between concentration and impairment. In addition to the consensus test battery subjects could also be examined using a driving simulator with scenarios sensitive to cannabis-related motor, sensory and/or cognitive effects. Analysis of findings would include a comparison of the effects of cannabis to alcohol on the same endpoints.

### Benzodiazepines (Alprazolam)

A second exemplar offered to illustrate the application of the tiered protocol is alprazolam, a frequently dispensed and abused, short-acting benzodiazepine medication that is primarily prescribed as an anxiolytic. The tiered approach would work as described below.

**Tier I: Pharmacological and toxicological review.** Alprazolam has been well characterized pharmacologically. It binds nonselectively to the benzodiazepine receptor complex site on the $GABA_A$ receptor and facilitates the binding of GABA. The presence of GABA inhibits the action of several connected brain structures. Sedation is reported to require only 15 to 16% receptor occupancy, which is readily achieved with a typical oral dose. The inhibition exerted by GABA results in a general slowing of brain activity. In addition, there is significant interaction with other neurotransmitter systems. Alprazolam is known to interact with serotonergic and noradrenergic pathways that contribute to its efficacy in the treatment of anxiety, but that could also potentially impair abilities critical to driving. Alprazolam has been studied in clinical trials relative to placebo, and other benzodiazepines and shown to cause significant sedation, somnolence, slurring of speech, abnormal coordination, and memory impairment, all of which are relevant to the five domains identified controlling driver performance. Alprazolam has also been assessed for its ability to interact with herbal products and other pharmaceuticals, which should be taken into account when assessing its risk to driving.

The clinical pharmacology of alprazolam was reviewed in a 2004 article by Verster and Volkerts. Current toxicology information for alprazolam, includes a report on the concentrations of scheduled prescription drugs in blood samples from people arrested in Sweden for driving under the influence of drugs over a 2-year period (Jones, Holgren, & Kugelberg, 2007). Diazepam and nordazepam were the most frequently identified drugs in the blood samples, followed by alprazolam (N=430; 5.6%). The authors reported that the drugged-driving subjects' concentrations of the benzodiazepines found in the blood samples to be higher than the generally-prescribed therapeutic doses.

There are no specific reports of signs and symptoms of alprazolam in impaired drivers who have been arrested and assessed. Based on an assessment of these considerations, there would be a basis to conclude that alprazolam should be further assessed epidemiologically and experimentally for its actual ability to impair driving.

**Tier II: Epidemiological review.** Epidemiological review for evidence of involvement of alprazolam in impaired driving populations, such as in deceased drivers would then be conducted. Alprazolam is a member of the benzodiazepine class of medications, which are well documented as having high frequency and prevalence in at-risk driving populations. The overall results of epidemiological studies investigating crash risk for this drug class of drugs has shown mixed results (Drummer et al, 2004). From the published data it is difficult to determine the crash risk for specific drugs within this class. Clearly there are marked differences depending upon whether the drug is short- or long-acting, and whether it is taken chronically or acutely. The findings of a recent, systematic review of epidemiological studies investigating benzodiazepines and road safety (Orriols, 2009), support the need for this drug to progress to the next tier of the assessment protocol.

**Tier III: Standardized behavioral assessment.** Alprazolam has been the subject of laboratory studies investigating the effect of the drug on the five behavioral domains relevant to driving. Impairment has been demonstrated on measures of all five domains: alertness/arousal (Kozená, Frantik, & Horváth, 1995) attention and processing speed (Snyder et al., 2005; Leufkens et al., 2007), reaction time/psychomotor functions (Leufkens et al., 2007), sensory-perceptual functions

(Vermeeren et al., 1995) and executive functions (Leufkens et al., 2007). In their review of the psychomotor effects of alprazolam, Verster and Volkerts (2004) included a wide range of tests that measure abilities not generally considered "psychomotor," including measures of attention, perceptual functioning, neurovestibular functioning and executive functions. They reported that at following an acute 1.0 mg dose, 84% of the "psychomotor performance" tests (from 38 different cited studies), showed "impairment." This kind of meta-analytic review demonstrates the need for a standardized behavioral assessment protocol. The 38 studies that were cited employed a range of tests of varying sensitivity and a range of testing methods. It would be far more useful to have information from a validated test battery of known sensitivity, all of which are measures of essential driving abilities. Rather than presenting a percentage of impaired tests, the results could be presented in terms of the severity of impairment across each of the five critical domains on a validated test battery relative to a well-known impairing drug such as alcohol.

In addition to these laboratory tests, alprazolam has also been studied using the Netherlands CBR Driving Test, 100-km highway driving method. Verster et al. (2002) found impairment of the ability to maintain lane position (i.e., the standard deviation of lateral position; SDLP) following a 1 mg dose of alprazolam to be comparable to a .15 g/dL alcohol level. In a more recent study, Leufkens et al. (2007) compared over-the-road driving performance of healthy volunteers after taking immediate and extended release formulations of alprazolam (1 mg). Both formulations impaired driving performance however the extended release was less impairing than the immediate release.

This example demonstrates, for alprazolam, that prior studies have addressed many of the pharmacological, epidemiological, toxicological, and behavioral questions needed to determine the extent to which the drug impairs driving. Clearly the results reviewed above show that alprazolam is a drug that impairs driving. However, the application of a standardized behavioral assessment protocol would better answer some of the specific questions related to the effects of dose, tolerance, and to better characterize the specific abilities impaired by the drug.

## Summary of the Panel's Findings

The view of the panel is that at present there is inadequate information to classify drugs into "driving risk" categories or to generate a list of drugs that are "safe" for driving. This deprives the public of information that could reduce the risk of drug-impaired driving. This issue is relevant for prescription and over-the-counter medications as well as for illicit drugs. The panel recommended the use of a protocol employing well established practices in toxicology, pharmacology and epidemiology to identify drugs or drug classes most or least likely to have an adverse effect on driving. This information would be used to prioritize drugs for standardized laboratory of cognitive, perceptual and motor functioning as well as driving tests. Specific recommendations for the design and validation of the behavioral assessment protocol were provided. Finally, communication of the findings of this effort to the public will require careful planning to maximize the potential benefits for driver safety.

### Findings

- Drivers need better information regarding the impact of medications and illicit drugs on their ability to safely operate motor vehicles.
- Current medication labels often warn that "this medication may cause drowsiness, use caution when driving." These labels do not specify the degree of crash risk associated with dose, time since drug administration, impact of acute versus steady-state use, interaction with other medications, etc., as factors to consider when making the decision to drive. The labels fail to communicate to the consumer or the prescriber the extent to which the drug impairs driving and increases the risk of crashing.
- For the vast majority of drugs, only limited pharmacological, epidemiological, and behavioral evidence is available indicating the extent to which they impair driving. At present, there is insufficient scientific information for generating a list of "safe medications."
- The consensus opinion of the panel was that methodologies currently exist that can be used to systematically evaluate the risk of driving impairment attributable to medications and illicit drugs.
- It was the panel's opinion that a standardized, validated protocol could be developed for assessing the impairing effect of prescription and over-the-counter medications as well as illicit drugs on driving related skills and abilities. Application of this protocol would better inform consumers, healthcare providers, and transportation operators of the potential impairment of driving resulting from the use of drugs.
- The panel has suggested a protocol for assessing the risk of driving impairment caused by prescription and over-the-counter medications and illicit drugs. The first phase of this tiered protocol is a pharmacological analysis, aimed at evaluating the extent to which a drug is likely to interfere with brain functions essential for driving. This is followed by analysis of epidemiological and toxicological data demonstrating the extent to which a drug has been found to be associated with crashes and injuries. The epidemiological and toxicological data would serve to identify the doses, time course, and concomitantly administered drugs (and alcohol) that have been associated with crashes. The next step in the protocol uses a validated behavioral test battery incorporating state-of-the-art assessment methods designed to evaluate the effect of drugs on behaviors essential for safe vehicle operation (EDAD model). In addition to specifying laboratory tests, the

panel provided guidelines for driving simulation testing, and for over-the-road naturalistic studies of driving performance.

## Future Steps

Application of the tiered assessment protocol beyond an initial validation sample may appear to be an overly ambitious undertaking. However, it should be remembered that a small group of drugs account for the majority of medication-based driver impairment. Sedating antihistamines, tricyclic antidepressants, centrally-acting analgesics, benzodiazepines, and muscle relaxants account for the bulk of this impairment. This group of drugs could be targeted for early assessment in with the protocol in order to make some rapid advances in product labeling (i.e., identifying the degree to which drugs impair driving), and allowing for better informed prescribing and safer use of medications by patients.

## Challenges in Developing a Protocol to Assess Drug-Related Driving Impairment.

Discussion by the panel identified some of the limitations and challenges to what can be accomplished by the protocol due to a myriad of potential dosing restrictions, potential drug-drug and drug-alcohol interactions, tolerance and pharmacokinetic considerations, ethical and economic issues. It is unlikely that the full range of dosing conditions (e.g., route, formulation, dosing interval, dose, and frequency of use) could be examined. Administering doses to subjects at levels common in abuse could not be conducted ethically. Determining the extent to which tolerance occurs and the extent to which tolerance diminishes driving impairment is critically important but difficult to evaluate empirically. Although drug withdrawal is recognized as an important contributor to impairment, it can only be studied in a very limited manner using current laboratory methods. Given the nearly infinite number of potential drug-drug and drug-alcohol interactions, it is recognized the protocol can only address a small number of these interactions. The panel appreciates that impairment that may be evident with acute dosing or during the first few weeks of drug administration may disappear with chronic administration. This further increases the cost and complexity of laboratory assessments.

The panel recognizes the fact that there are significant inter-individual differences in how a drug is metabolized. A safe dose for one individual may result in toxic levels in another (especially among older patients). Large numbers of subjects would have to be tested to fully appreciate these inter-individual differences.

In spite of these challenges, there are very clear benefits to proceeding with the protocol, and marked disadvantages of continuing with the status quo. Although imperfect, the information that is potentially provided by the application of the protocol should result in more reliable and valid information than has been previously available to prescribers and consumers.

# References

American Psychological Association, & National Council on Measurement in Education. (1999). *Standards for Educational and Psychological Testing.* Washington, DC: American Educational Research Association.

Bever, Jr., C. T., Grattan, L., Panitch, H. S., & Johnson, K. P. (1995). The brief repeatable battery of neuropsychological tests for Multiple Sclerosis: A preliminary serial study. *Multiple Sclerosis, 1,*165–169.

Bossong, M. G., van Berckel, B. N., Boellaard, R., Zuurman, L., Schuit, R. C., Windhorst, A. D., van Gerven, J. M., Ramsey, N. F., Lammertsma, A. A., & Kahn, R. S. (2009). Delta 9-tetrahydrocannabinol induces dopamine release in the human striatum. *Neuropsychopharmacology, 34,* 759-766.

Brown, T., Dow, B., Marshall, D., & Allen, S. (2007). Validation of stopping and turning behavior for novice drivers in the National Advanced Driving Simulator. *Proceedings of the National Driving Simulation Conference.* Iowa City, IA. Retrieved from http://www.nads-sc.uiowa.edu/dscna07/DSCNA07CD/main.htm

Couper, F. J., & Logan, B. K. (2004). *Drugs and human performance fact sheets.* (DOT HS 809725). Washington, D.C: National Highway Traffic Safety Administration.

Drummer, O. H., Gerostamoulos, J., Batziris, H., Chu, M., Caplehorn, J., Robertson, M.D., & Swann, P. (2004). The involvement of drugs in drivers of motor vehicles killed in Australian road traffic crashes. *Accident Analysis & Prevention, 36,* 239-248.

Fleishman, E. A., Quaintance, M. K., & Broedling, L. A. (1984). *Taxonomies of human performance: The description of human tasks.* Orlando, FL: Academic Press.

Gurtman, C. G., Broadbear, J. H., & Redman, J. R. (2008). Effects of modafinil on simulator driving and self-assessment of driving following sleep deprivation. *Human Psychopharmacology: Clinical and Experimental, 23,* 681-692.

International Conference on Harmonisation. (2005, November). *Efficacy Guidelines.* Retrieved from http://www.ich.org/cache/compo/276-254-1.html

Jones, A. W., Holgren, A., & Kugelberg, F. C. (2007). Concentrations of scheduled prescription drugs in blood of impaired drivers: Considerations for interpreting the results. *Ther Drug Monit  29,* 248-260.

Jones, R. K., Shinar, D., & Walsh, J. M. (2003). *State of knowledge of drug-impaired driving.* (DOT HS 809 642). Washington, D.C.: National Highway Traffic Safety Administration. Retrieved from http://icsw.nhtsa.gov/people/injury/research/stateofknwlegedrugs/stateofknwlegedrugs/.

Kay, G. G., Michaels, M. A., & Pakull, B. (2009). Simulated driving changes in young adults with ADHD receiving mixed amphetamine salts extended release and atomoxetine. *Journal of Attention Disorders*, *12*, 316-329.

Kozená, L., Frantik, E., & Horváth, M. (1995). Vigilance impairment after a single dose of benzodiazepines. *Psychopharmacology*, *119*, 39-45.

Lacey, J. H., Kelly-Baker, T., Furr-Holden, D, Voas, R. B., Romano, E., Ramirez, A., Brainard, K., Moore, C., Torres, P., & Berning, A. (2009). *2007 National roadside survey of alcohol and drug use by drivers: Drug results* (DOT HS 811 249). Washington, DC: National Highway Traffic Safety Administration. Retrieved from http://www.nhtsa.gov/DOT/NHTSA/Traffic%20Injury%20Control/Articles/Associated% 20Files/811249.pdf.

Leufkens, T. R. M., Vermeeren, A., Smink, B. E., Van Ruitenbeek, P., & Ramaekers, J. G. (2007). Cognitive, psychomotor and actual driving performance in healthy volunteers after immediate and extended release formulations of Alprazolam 1 mg. *Psychopharmacology*, *191*, 951-959.

Lezak, M. D. (2004). *Neuropsychological assessment* (4th ed.). New York: Oxford University Press.

Maes, V., Charlier, C., Grenez, O., & Verstraete, A. (1999). Drugs and medicines that are suspected to have a detrimental impact on road user performance (Status P). *ROSITA*. Belgium: European Transport Commission.

National Institute on Drug Abuse (2007, February). *Commonly abused drugs.*Bethesda, MD: National Institute on Drug Abuse. Retrieved from http://www.nida.nih.gov/PDF/CADChart.pdf

National Transportation Safety Board. (2000). Safety Recommendation 1-00-1 through -4. Retrieved from http://www.ntsb.gov/pressrel/2000/000105.htm

Nuechterlein, K.H., et al. (2008). The                Consensus Cognitive        , Part 1: selection, reliability, and validity. *American Journal of Psychiatry*, *165*, 203–213.

Orriols, L., Salmi, L.-R., Philip, P., Moore, N., Delorme, B., Castot, A., & Lagarde, E. (2009). The impact of medicinal drugs on traffic safety: a systematic review of epidemiological studies. *Pharmacoepidemiology and Drug Safety, 18, 647-658*. Retrieved from http://www.ncbi.nlm.nih.gov/pmc/articles/PMC2780583/?tool=pubmed

Salaani, M. K., Heydinger, G. J., & Grygier, P. A. (2006). Measurement and modeling of tire forces on a low coefficient surface (2006-01-0559). Washington, DC: SAE International.

Senserrick, T. M., Brown, T., Quistberg, B. A., Marshall, D., & Winston, F. K. (2007). Validation of simulated assessment of teen driver speed management on rural roads.

*Annual Proceedings of the Association for the Advancement of Automotive Medicine, 51,* 525-536.

Shinar, D. (2005, June). Drug effects and their significance for traffic safety. *Transportation Research Circular, E-C096,* 52-64.

Snyder, P. J., Werth, J., Giordani, B., Caveney, A. F., Feltner, D., & Maruff, P. (2005). A method for determining the magnitude of change across different cognitive functions in clinical trials: The effects of acute administration of two different doses alprazolam. *Human Psychopharmacology Clinical and Experimental, 20,* 263-273

Staner, L., Ertie, S., Boeijinga, P., Rinaudo, G., Arnal, M. A., Muzet, A., & Luthringer, R. (2005). Next-day residual effects of hypnotics in DSM-IV primary insomnia: A driving simulator study with simultaneous electroencephalogram monitoring. *Psychopharmacology, 181,* 790-798.

Staplin, L., Lococo, K. H., Gish, K. W., & Martell, C. (2008). *A pilot study to test multiple medication usage and driving functioning.* (DOT HS 810 980). Washington, D.C: National Highway Traffic Safety Administration. Retrieved from http://ntl.bts.gov/lib/30000/30200/30265/810980.pdf.

Vermeeren, A., Jackson, J. L., Muntjewerff, N. D., Quint P. J., Harrison, E. M., & O'Hanlon, J. F. (1995). Comparison of acute alprazolam (0.25, 0.50 and 1.0 mg) effects versus those of lorazepam 2 mg and placebo on memory in healthy volunteers using laboratory and telephone tests. *Psychopharmacology, 118,* 1-9.

Verster, J. C., & Volkerts, E. R. (2004). Antihistamines and driving ability: Evidence from on-the-road driving studies during normal traffic. *Annals of Allergy, Asthma & Immunology, 92,* 294–305, 355.

Verster, J. C., Volkerts, E. C., & Verbaten, M. N. (2002). Effects of alprazolam on driving ability, memory functioning and psychomotor performance. *Neuropsychopharmacology, 27,* 260-269.

Verster, J.C., Wester, A.E., Goorden, M., van Wieringen, J.P., Olivier, B., & Volkerts, E. R. (2009). Novice drivers' performance after different alcohol dosages and placebo in the divided-attention steering simulator (DASS). *Psychopharmacology, 204,* 127-133.

Walsh, J. M., Verstraete, A. G., Huestis, M. A., & Morland, J. (2008). Guidelines for research on drugged driving. *Addiction, 103,* 1258-1268.

# Appendix A
## Consensus Test Battery for Assessing Impaired Driving Abilities

**Alertness/Arousal**
- Self-Report: visual analog scales, sleepiness scales
- Laboratory Performance Measures: tests of vigilance
- Sleep Laboratory Measures: physiological measures of sleep onset latency and ability to maintain wakefulness
- Driving Simulator: measures of ability to maintain speed and lane position on a 40+ minute driving scenario

**Attention and Processing Speed**
- Laboratory Performance Measures: tests of working memory, vigilance, focused attention, shifting attention, and divided attention
- Driving Simulator/Instrumented Vehicle: measures of eye movement and gaze, divided attention, and reaction time to crash likely events

**Reaction Time/Psychomotor Function**
- Laboratory Performance Measures: measures of choice/ complex reaction time, upper motor speed and coordination
- Driving Simulator/Instrumented Vehicle: brake reaction time tests, and steering measures (e.g., steering variability)

**Sensory-Perceptual Function**
- Laboratory Performance Measures: tests of visual fields, perimetry testing, and contrast sensitivity testing

**Executive Function**
- Laboratory Performance Measures: tests of mental flexibility, adaptive problem solving, abstract reasoning, impulse control, risk taking/risk assessment, organizational ability (including visuospatial organization), and planning
- Driving Simulator/Instrumented Vehicle: measures of navigational performance

# Appendix B
# Expert Panel Members

**Doug Beirness, Ph.D.**
Senior Research and Policy Analyst and Advisor
Canadian Centre on Substance Abuse
dbeirness@ccsa.ca

**Gary G. Kay, Ph.D.**
President
Cognitive Research Corporation
gkay@cogres.com

**Barry K. Logan, Ph.D., DABFT**
Director of Toxicological Services
NMS Labs
barry.logan@nms.labs.com

**Herbert Moskowitz, Ph.D.**
Professor Emeritus
California State University and
  University of California, Los Angeles
herbmosk@ucla.edu

**Jan Ramaekers, Ph.D.**
Head and Associate Professor
Department of Neuropsychology and
  Psychopharmacology
Faculty of Psychology and Neuroscience
Maastricht University
The Netherlands
j.raemakers@psychology.unimaas.nl

**Lionel Raymon, Pharm.D., Ph.D.**
Voluntary Assistant Professor
Department of Pathology
Forensic Toxicology Laboratory
Miller School of Medicine
University of Miami
lionelraymon@bellsouth.net

**Gordon S. Smith, M.D., M.P.H.**
Professor
Department of Epidemiology and Preventive
  Medicine
School of Medicine
University of Maryland
National Study Center for Trauma and EMS
gssmith@som.umaryland.edu

**Loren Staplin, Ph.D.**
Managing Partner
TransAnalytics, LLC
lstaplin@transanalytics.com

www.ingramcontent.com/pod-product-compliance
Lightning Source LLC
Chambersburg PA
CBHW081814280526
45789CB00008B/3122